CHANGE, CREATI\
AND HOPE I!
CALLED PANᴅ......

uncertainty
fear
perspective
& prayer

POETRY AND SHORT STORIES
BY NORTH CAROLINA WRITERS
MEMBERS OF WRITING BOOTCAMP CHARLOTTE

outskirts
press

Editor's Note

On May 2, 2020 — during the height of the world's coronavirus pandemic, I asked participants of Writing Bootcamp/Charlotte — a six-month creative writing program — to create pieces for a book about how they were impacted — personally, professionally, emotionally, socially - by the crisis.

With no specific topics in mind, but with all of us aware of the unprecedented time in modern history, I asked the writers to share their feelings in short stories, opinion columns or poetry.

Within a day, most of the 11 writers accepted the challenge. Then, came the difficult part — they had to write. Most of these pieces were written in May and June 2020. Many of them were written before the death of George Floyd in Minnesota and the national protests.

In early June, I asked each writer to create a story or poem about love and how it factors into the triple crisis - pandemic, racial unrest and economic turmoil.

To know the writers is to know an eclectic, diverse group. Several had little creative writing experience. Others gave up writing years ago because life got in the way or they allowed naysayers to quell their creativity. Three members of the group are published authors.

Most of the group lives in the Charlotte area. The nod, however, goes to Doreen Day, who I met at a writing workshop in Asheville in 2019. She drove from Henderson County (216 miles roundtrip) to attend our three-hour Saturday classes in Charlotte.

Enjoy. This is what Writing Bootcamp members had to say.

Some items include graphic language, depicting fear, uncertainty, loss and survival. With a mixture of grief and hope, each writer sought comfort in their own words.

* Editor Glenn Proctor. Formatting, cover design and additional editing by author, marketing professional and bootcamp member Trish Stukbauer.

SOW YOUR ART, SOW IT SHORT...

Glenn Proctor

Blaze your blank pages with journey and grit
Love fresh frenetic; twisted passion of write;
Simple words uncovered in naked letters
Creativity found before blocks hid your light.

Gather, put best of imagination together
In bold revealing acts of raw common sense
Doomed, first topic dead, come and gone
Think? Let absolute sure writing commence.

Energy, with truth can be told in a few;
Long stilted writing might just be a sin.
Let sentences thrive, with no more, or no less.
Good stories have heft; let creative writing begin.

Sow your sound words for purpose and art
Sentences got verve; with meanings so strong
There's wind and sway in descriptions so sweet.
Write short or scoff when rewrite calls it long.

The Writers

Lizz Baxter – An Army veteran of Operation Iraqi Freedom in 2002, she comes from a small Nebraska railroad town. Writing from a young age through the encouragement of her grandmother, Lizz tells stories of her adventures around the world and as a young female soldier. Arriving in Charlotte in 2012, she serves the community and fellow veterans as a real estate broker. When she is not working with clients, she is shooting and editing video footage, attempting yoga handstands, roller skating, exploring Charlotte's secret places, supporting local businesses or out for long walks and bike rides with her husband, Monte.

Jeffrey Bryant – A former Army Airborne Ranger, he graduated from West Point with a Bachelor of Science degree in literature. Jeff presented President Barrack Obama with a West Point Battle Ring in 2014 before deploying in support of Operation Inherent Resolve as a platoon leader in 2015. He advocates for the Burning Man Project, an arts community constructed perennially in Black Rock City, Nevada. Jeff writes poetry and studies theology, Jungian psychology and appreciates the healing nature of art as it helps make sense of our current world.

Carla Carlisle – A speaker and mental health advocate, she penned her first memoir, Journey to the Son, to prompt discussions about the impact of trauma on children. A member of Alpha Kappa Alpha Sorority, Inc, she received an undergraduate degree in sociology from Indiana University in Bloomington, a master's degree in human resources management from American University in Washington, D.C. and another graduate degree in organizational development from Johns Hopkins University in Baltimore. Carla is active with several mental health organizations and is an active volunteer with Mental Health America of Central Carolinas.

Doreen Day – Doreen admits that her discovery of writing is a recent endeavor that has become a passion. An avid reader, her goal is to create provocative work through inspired thought and exceptional research. Saying her work comes from life experience and exquisite detail, her creativity extends to stained glass and drawing. A former partner in a title insurance company for 25 years, Doreen has a deep affinity for animals, especially greyhounds that she has rescued and rehabilitated for three decades. A massage therapist and Reiki Master-practitioner, the Catskills Mountains of New York native resides in Western North Carolina.

Sara Dir – Born in Serbia, raised in Canada and living in the United States since 17, Sara's vivacious and resilient spirit has equipped her to live and survive through many seasons of life. Since childhood, she has used creative writing to relate to the world, using it to channel interests in art, poetry, philosophy and the human condition. Vivid dreamer, motivational speaker, passionate leader and foreign student advocate, immigrant, Sara strives to enrich others through her writing. In August, Sara will receive an MBA from Queens University.

Jim Dukes – A civil engineer by trade, Jim turned to photography and healing art as a vocation after a 20-year career in engineering, explosive ordinance disposal and multiple traumatic brain injuries. He has completed projects in 30 states and eight countries. The former artist in residence at Tapp's Art Center in Columbia, SC, and past director of the Healing Arts Programs at the Big Barn Retreat in Blythwood, SC, he taught healing arts and photography to Army drill sergeants, active duty military, veterans and military family members. In 2017, he completed a TEDx talk on the power of healing art for veterans. Still a professional photographer and artist, he is executive director of the Charlotte Art League, a large gallery and studio space in the city's NODA district.

Lori Myers – A writer of short stories and poetry, her offerings have appeared in the literary magazines of Belmont Abbey College and Montreat College. She is working on several reminiscent short stories honoring lost loved ones. Words used to describe her by those who know her best: authentic, inspiring, passionate, driven, compassionate, empathetic, committed, leader, persistent, dedicated, tenacious and effervescent. Lori is also a coach focused on the professional advancement of women in technology.

Amy Campbell Pratt – A later graduate, Cum Laude, from UNC-Charlotte with a Bachelor of Arts in Psychology. She has spent the last 25 years as a media creator for Fortune 500 companies. She's an actor, a drummer, photographer, Reiki Master and professional creative coach. Her mission is to help others love the artist within themselves, to find their superpowers. Her first book *"Speaking of Radial Tires; SORTing Out a Purpose Through the Random Chaos of Life; A Raw Collection of Photos and Prose"* is set for release in November 2020. To learn more, visit her website lovingtheARTISTwithin.com

Glenn Proctor – Instructor, **WRITING BOOTCAMP/Charlotte**; author of five books and manuscript editor, executive coach, mental health and suicide prevention trainer, 40 year-journalist, Pulitzer Prize winner, Pulitzer Prize judge, Marine gunnery sergeant and Vietnam veteran. Glenn writes from lived experience: foster kid, single parent, alcoholic and disabled veteran. A victim of Agent Orange poisoning, he is a diabetic and a prostate cancer survivor.

Kimberly Shelton – A native Texan & former military brat now residing in Charlotte. She's a fun-loving, dance-until-you-drop kind of gal. She adores all things animal & is a parent to those with paws. Reading, writing, dancing & yoga captivate her interest. She's enchanted with Motown, R&B, soul, funk & jazz. She's a wanna-be mosaic artist. She resonates with the raw & emotional, so whenever you read her writing a piece of her heart remains with you always.

Trish Stukbauer – An author, recovering journalist and multi-platform communications professional, she is editor of *Showtime Car Culture*, a former newspaper and real estate magazine editor and director of communications for Holy Comforter Church in Charlotte. As owner of i.e. marketing, she works with clients ranging from an international business incubator and globally recognized home décor retailer to advertising agencies on both coasts, non-profit organizations (CNE, CDE, CNC), businesses, authors and celebrities.

Andrea Towner – Director of Development for Mental Health America of Central Carolinas in Charlotte, she finds fulfillment by engaging volunteers, donors and partners in the work of promoting mental wellness and preventing suicide. Andrea, with an English degree from Virginia Tech, loves writing to share inspirational stories and calls to action. She and her husband, Doug, are the parents of two adult sons and a puppy named Cleo.

Diane Weekley – Board Certified Coach and long-time storyteller, Diane believes in the power of myth and story to shape lives. With a focus on real personal connection – for herself and others – Diane uses exemplary communication and lifestyle tools to repair and restore relationships. In addition to her coaching practice, Diane works with Charlotte-based Veterans Bridge Home to support veterans and help military families transition successfully to civilian life. In her leisure time, she enjoys reading fantasy fiction, karate nights and exploring life with family and grandchildren.

The Work

Lizz Baxter

The following story titled, "Two Full Moons" explores two global pandemic perspectives from an American lens with an Eastern spin.

The Yin and Yang ancient Chinese philosophy is a concept of dualism.

Opposite forces are thought to be complementary, interconnected and interdependent in the natural world.

The lunar calendar represents the passing of time as well as an 'outside looking in' Man on the Moon viewpoint.

The original piece is to be read in a circle to create a dizzying disoriented feeling to the reader.

The global crisis is described by the young and old as life changing and we for once agree that life will never be the same again.

TWO FULL MOONS

Lizz Baxter

Two Full Moons – Gift of Time - Global Swoon – Mother Nature Realign

Impending Doom – Realities Intertwine - Uncertainty Blooms

Examination of Minds – Connectivity Booms

Yang

Two full moons ago a sickness infected the land. Currency couldn't pay the demand. Public confusion spread. Nations invent their own solutions. Hysteria guided by unfounded logic. Fresh foods rot on shelves. Empty syringes of distraction. Fate is accepted only when depressed celebrities tell the people how to think and feel. Type A's drop status from couches. While overscheduled offspring enjoy fresh air. Freed imaginations fill empty streets. Extinct teens reemerge. The beautiful people begrudgingly escape their hamster wheels.

Commerce somehow remains alive only for those who serve the masses. Fabricated food at fingertips. Complaints persist. Suffering overshadowed by shameless plugs. Carefully constructed messaging distracts and denies. Failed States. Insatiable Greed. Vulnerable populations drop like flies. Polished politicians look out their windows untouched by discomfort. No time for reflection. Hurry toward confusion. IV drips of interruption are cut. Drowsy eyes open slowly. Experiences and life's fragility are unveiled. United through struggle.

The talking heads cross their fingers in hope that personal arsenals will remain contained.

Yin

Two full moons ago the globe began to heal. Holistic wellness. Not Band-Aids covering gaping wounds. Stitching the social gaps while flashing signs hum in silence. Nature prepared a lesson plan. Survival lifts the fog enough to see beyond noses' end. Alliances form. Cables connect. Waves of kindness lap at shore's edge.

We the People. Power in numbers. Togetherness apart. Effort made. Keep the Peace. Laugh more. Homeostasis disrupted. Dust off old treasures. Resurrect youthful Play. Reacquaint with modern luxury. Muted Privilege. Forgotten illuminated. Beauty emerges uncovered. No longer overshadowed by chaos. Aid encouraged from full pockets. Human kind begins to see our choices. Frightened or Enlightened? Living everyday like the last.

SPONTANEOUS ENCOUNTERS

Lizz Baxter

Will spontaneous encounters await on the other side of masks? Or, will it become a novelty? Will we share seats and laugh at mutually relevant jokes? Will happy hour ever spill over into unplanned friendships again?

Order in advance. Plan ahead. Hurry! Choose your food from perfectly curated photos. I wonder if in the future, you can lick them? Do they normally charge for ketchup?

Thought bubbles pop overhead as I stand in line for take out. Thoughts too deep for sharing. It's our anniversary. No restaurants. No ambiance. No dinner plates. No crystal goblets.

Only squeaky Styrofoam. I cringe each time I squash them into the bin. Biodegradable is impossible.

Our favorite takeout spot. How romantic? Maybe, curbside ice cream? Dine-in options are eliminated along with our environmentally conscious choices. Move forward. I sense someone impatiently shifting their weight back and forth. In a hurry to go "no damn where..."

Back to my thought bubbles. I can usually see my waitress smile. Is she still a waitress? What is her new title? It's my turn. I smile warmly under my mask.

I wonder if she noticed. She didn't.

No money exchanged. I paid online. Apple Pay.

No time for chit chat, there is money to be made. Muffled words exchanged self consciously. The voice in my ears is extra loud. Consonants jumble. Phrases repeated. The exchange is over. Next person...?

Frustrated and embarrassed, we walk home to our couches. Spontaneous moment lost.

WHAT IF... LOVE?

Lizz Baxter

What if Love... could drown hate?
Heal wounds, give rescue breaths of life,
Clean hearts, souls and minds
In a tsunami of kindness.

What if Love... gave us amnesia?
Retaining only good memories
Clouding bad, leaving only lessons learned
In a hurricane of understanding.

What if Love... allowed for forgiveness?
Setting all captives free
Clearing life's painful past, starting fresh and new path
In a tornado of justice.

What if Love... infected us all?
Empathy spreading like invisible particles
Changing our DNA
In a virus of compassion.

Evolution

Lizz Baxter

One of my guilty pleasures, especially when stressed and tired, is BBC's Planet Earth series narrated by David Attenborough. A British accent combined with ambient background soundtracks is as soothing as it gets. I sink into the couch, wrapped in my favorite blanket, and watch creatures navigate life in their natural habitat. I sit back and relax while learning from the masters of survival. Some creatures look familiar and others are strange, prehistoric, and downright U-G-L-Y. These creatures live in and overcome the harshest environments to make way for life. Death is around every corner, and starvation is inevitable. Yet, life finds a way.

Did you know that fish can live 1 KM below the surface of the ocean under tons of pressure and create their own luminescence to capture prey? These creatures have never seen the sunlight, yet they survive. They have physically evolved, meeting the conditions of their surroundings. Some have tennis ball size eyes. Others have glowing transparent goo atop of their head in lieu of eyes to see upward. Adaptability at its finest. Millenia of fine-tuning and uncomfortable change. It really gets me thinking, if this is possible in an undiscovered, untouched world; what is possible in our own world? I ask myself this daily during the pandemic quarantine when hopelessness creeps in. Setbacks have historically been overcome even in the direst situations. Nature corrects itself, and a new life emerges. We get to be part of this natural phenomenon. It isn't always clear and it certainly isn't pretty. Maybe it's time to shed our old self to make room for a new one. Maybe we can approach each new day like a luminescent fish and create our own light.

We must overcome! It's not easy but it is worth it. You are stronger than you have ever known yourself to be. You are experiencing an evolution.

THE DEVIL YOU KNOW

Jeffrey Bryant

When it is time to go,

don't let the devil know.

A little schoolhouse,

East of Eden sits a man,

cold, blank as a slate.

Eyes dark and full

of buzzards.

Smoke blots out the sun

over schoolyards quieted

like courtrooms.

Residue from a fire burning,

embers low and slow.

Mothers prayed.

The blackboard

reads 100 times:

Look in the shadows.

QUIET RABBIT

Jeffrey Bryant

No voice or time to ask, why God?

What's with all this suffering?

Briar patch soul

rich with love.

Spiritual side

one must sew

grow to hide.

Young soul,

verge of dying.

Met anyone

whom death consumed?

Burn a candle

feel the tingling

in one's spine.

Ancient's banging

drums, waking

lost souls.

Built a fire in all that dark,

so the dead can feel eternal heat.

Quit bothering the minstrel heap.

NOT FROM HERE

Jeffrey Bryant

Not here

talking, hearing, brimming,

pissing, moaning.

100 reasons not

to give.

Give until it kills you.

Opposite happens.

Fear no thing.

Mindful powers of heroes;

Legends supernatural

Members, part of you.

---◆---

Went to see the minstrel every Monday and Wednesday for coffee and wisdom.

Although minstrel was not this man's profession, teaching novice creatures was his purpose for living.

Like Proteus of mythology, taking the shape of a gentleman I know to deliver the keys of the universe, if inquired properly.

---◆---

THE MINSTREL

Jeffrey Bryant

Man said, look here, old boy,
I am YOU. My shop's a mess.
Won't you help me organize this?

Nodding and picking up Emmitt
Smith's rookie card, I smiled.

That's worth a fortune, said the wise man.
Most of this is trash, however.

Leafing through stacks of newspapers and
shelves of books, every nook and cranny,
ions rushed blood to my fingertips.

One gold parchment shined from below
a pile of nothing. Shining mysteriously,
saying quietly in my ear, I am YOU.
Raising the papyrus to my eye,
my body and clothes hit the floor,
however, my soul joined nothing-ness.

The old man started an old record, smiling and
humming into the abyss.

LOVE'S A BLACK DOG

Jeffrey Bryant

Sitting loyally, equidistant,

    painfully whimpering in shared pools of our anxiety.

Darkness falls, peace lingers dreaming,

    the little black dog ensures its warmth finds mine, making

    damn sure it can feel me, wonders gods feel in us humans. Grieving

    what's still living terminable.

Sun bathing in position of the Sphinx,

    watching Sun death and resurrection,

    rustling birds and wondrous things fluttering about in mystical

    ecstasy, eye slits dozing into perfect darkness.

Then Sunday came. Men in white coats rang the bell, saying "There, there"

    like old lady witch doctors,

    took me to the white-washed asylum.

The dog was left at the door.

THROUGH MY WINDOW

Carla A. Carlisle

I sit looking outside my window and see nature. From this view, all is well with the world. Trees, grass, flowers, bushes wet and nourished… drop by drop.

My boys are in the other room. I hear them playing video games after a full day of academics, followed by dinner and now it's the guys' time. The rain interrupted the basketball game out front. Hey! Even I hoop with them sometime.

Our home could be any other household, but it is not. I am the mother of young Black Kings in a country where being black can mean "less than" or "get cha dead" and we are in the midst of a pandemic.

My thoughts change from nature to my boys. What are their odds of living? Striving? Thriving? They've already beaten some odds, so I should be encouraged. So, why does that drip drop of worry become a full on downpour of anxiety?

I turn on the television and see another black man dead, a little black girl handcuffed at school. Where am I?

I pour experiences into my young men, show love and affection, and try to balance reality with faith, hopes and dreams.

My job is to be patient, kind, real and a role model. All I want to be is a Mom whose boys grow into men, to leave a legacy for the future, to move the needle forward.

Expect much?

Well yes, I do.

THOSE EYES

Carla A. Carlisle

Every night I look into his eyes.

They say eyes are the windows to the soul

So true.

His eyes caught my soul, my breath, my heart...

I melted.

He opened those big brown eyes. My heart stopped.

Never saw such beautiful eyes, flecks of hazel, sometimes gray;

The color far less noticed than their innocence.

People stared wherever we went.

He was *King*, hypnotizing with those eyes.

This morning I realized that my manchild was in danger.

Hated. Feared. Betrayed by a people and country he might one day
    be called to protect.

The preemie destined to death escaped it, only to exist in a time
    when his chocolate skin and those eyes...

Once met with adoring stares... now make him look angry.

Aggressive.

Scary.

MY SECRET

Carla A. Carlisle

It's been years since you became my escape from reality.

You walked past me, I reached out. Something I never do.

I was divorced, discouraged and feeling well… not sexy.

I made a pledge; I wouldn't go without *IT* again.

Your job – help me heal.

Your dark chocolate skin, your rod, your groove, your vibe, your flow.

It's everything.

You, young'n, have taught me plenty. My secret sauce, fantasy in a jar.

It's remarkable having earth shattering, sheet-grabbing, laugh and

shed a tear eruptions! We are in double digits now, bro.

You rang? Here I come. Enough chit-chat.

Let's get it. Soaked bed sheets. I'm spent.

Tired, yes! Pleased, absolutely!

We done good! Love you?

Sure, but don't tell nobody.

You're mine, a personal treasure.

WEEKS ON END

Doreen Day

Twelve weeks ago, I held your hand. Walked beside you. Laughed.

Bumped shoulders. Goofy. New beginnings. Call me!

Eleven weeks ago, I inhaled your essence. Musky. You shine.

Can't wait for our next meeting. Text me!

Ten weeks ago, we are lovers. Promise weaves as limbs tangle.

Dreams roll. Sunlight strokes soft skin. Steamed mirror.

I love you as water pools. Nine weeks ago, our first spat. Over what?
Nothing? Something?

I'm sorry! Me too! Cool air wafts. Spring peepers sing. Warm hands
explode.

Eight weeks ago, I held you tight. Shed tears from your cheek.

Salted drops hugged my fingers. Our souls shook.

There's a bad boy in town. Slick. Brutal. No mercy.

Covid doesn't matter who you are. Sickness. Death.

Lockdown. I can't touch you. Distanced. You can't hug me.

I can't die alone.

SEEDED QUESTIONS

Doreen Day

Tuesday morning, clouds, I sip coffee and gaze out the window.

Brilliant rose-breasted gross beak lands on the railing, spreading

wings, swooping seed…

I wonder my feathered friend, if I were to ask if you care that

Millions are sick and thousands continue to die from the coronavirus, would you show compassion?

Would you show compassion to those who struggle with worry for their loved ones? Would you wrap your wings around children who have lost parents and are now alone?

Would you show empathy to those family members who could not be with their loved ones during death? Would you offer solace that the dead are now at peace from pain?

Would you share your daily food with others who are poor? Those who have pangs of hunger in their bellies and loneliness in their hearts?

Would you offer comfort to the elderly who sit alone in the dark waiting for the wrath to reach their door, as moans of pain and coughs spew the virus in the air?

Would you have the strength to lead a country with pure heart and wisdom? Accept knowledge of others for the best of a nation's people. To lead its people to make wise decisions, care for others and understand the impact of this killer on friends, strangers and themselves?

Yes, you would. You don't know greed. You don't know politics.

SLOW GLIDE

Doreen Day

Shaky hands envelop her rosary. Darkness. Distant coughs. She waits.

Anticipating. What will it look like when it comes?

Sunlight pushes. Gnarly fingers button. Soft knock. Caregiver and breakfast.

Morning Miss Edna!" Fuchsia mask, eyes smile. "Are you the virus?"

"Oh, no, Miss Edna. This is to protect you. Remember? For your safety."

Rocker creaks slow glide. Pictures once treasured hang dusty.

Giggles in the hall. Soft knock. "Hi Edna!" Craggy body grips a flashy red walker.

"It's me, Norm!" Silence. Strained recollection. Memory triggers.

"Yes... Norm, hello."

"Evenin' Miss Edna. Time for your pills."

Thick glasses magnify dark, gentle eyes.

"Remember me? Jason" adjusting her pillow. Tucks her in.

Eyes fixed on black mask.

"Lights out now." "Are you..." door closes.

Shadow crosses pale light from her window

Shaky hands once again envelop the rosary. Beads rattle.

Cross warms. The faint whisper questions...

"Are you the virus?"

SUBLIMAL

Doreen Day

Make no mistake, though Caucasian, the blood of my sisters and brothers,
flows freely through my veins.
Tribal voices echo strong.
Ancient ways rumble my soul.
I dream of a massive ball of fire. I run for refuge. Enraged flames lash at
my heels. Heart pounds. Sweat soaked sheets twist and I am trapped.
Still alive.
On reservations 'generally given' by the United States, people die. Not
enough their land and way of life, massacred and desecrated? Strangers
forced their religion and arrogance upon the indigenous.
Who were – and are – the real savages?
Covid-19, ball of fire in my dream. Killing my brothers and sisters.
No fresh water to clean. Children hungry. Elders die. Families struggle.
Medical shortages. Dust rolls barren plains. Promised, given nothing.

FOOL TALK!

HOKEY OR NOT… It's the Truth

Doreen Day

Covid-19, an acute pandemic. Harsh. It will pass.

Humanity injustice. Still infecting. Still affecting.

Chronic history speaks symptoms:

Racism. Sexism.

Religious Indifference. Homelessness.

Veterans disrespected. Elderly discarded.

Children hungry. Animal cruelty.

Political corruption. Environmental destruction.

Substance abuse. Suicide personified.

Education enabled. Healthcare flatlines.

AMERICA'S CAUSE OF DEATH: greed, control, twisted ego, abuse of power, intolerance, corruption, complacency, empty promises, hatred, fear.

I believe.

Reincarnation of a nation. It's people rising above.

I believe.

We can live. We can love. We can breathe.

DEFINITION?

Sara Dir

What is love?
Is it the numbness that I feel in my bones?
Or, the stillness I find around me,
Suddenly,
After crying until all tears have dried
       from the ducts of my eyes?

Is it the comforting quiet I feel?
After my mind has been racing for hours,
Like a raging horse in the summer heat,
       tormenting me.

Finally,
I can taste the moment for what it is,
A sober serenity,
An evergreen of tranquility;
The peace of finally answering the cries
       of one's inner self,
And loving oneself,
       tenderly,
       unconditionally...

THE EDGE: Freedom

Sara Dir

I need someone to listen. I feel so utterly hopeless with myself.

There's a war waging within me and just when I think it's finally over, and that I'm making progress, the war reemerges.

I keep fighting because deep down there's a will stronger than myself, perhaps God's will, that won't allow me to give up. At moments, I find myself wondering if I am stronger than I think, why do I feel so weak? At times, I feel I'm falling into a hole.

And, I'm going to share something with you that nobody knows.

I was sitting on the 30th floor of a friend's apartment today and thought, only for a moment, what it would be like if I jumped off the balcony.

My fear of heights no longer mattered and I could visualize myself climbing over the railing. I could feel the rush of blood traveling from the top of my head to the bottom of my feet; the feeling of flightless flying.

What if I could finally stop this feeling of depression?

Something took over me and I could feel myself wanting to get up, but then I became conscious of my breath and the "ground" beneath me.

"Out of my depth, lost in the air...", the words of a song came to mind, resonated, bringing me back to reality. I realized that true freedom begins in one's mind and this freedom is worth the fight necessary to achieve it.

Therefore, I live on.

TP (haiku)

Sara Dir

Soft and white as snow
Distant as the clouds above
Scarcity – man's plague.

POSSIBILITY (haiku)

Sara Dir

Light shines through dark waves

As hope emerges firmly –

Push beyond limits.

HOWLS of 2020

Sara Dir

I hug my pillow a little closer tonight

Contemplating the dawn of a new decade,

An era segregated by thought, color, emotion…

A perplexing time stung by fear and uncertainty.

An infectious virus sweeps the earth

Mercilessly claiming the lives of innocents in its path;

Cries of BLM protestors thunder through the streets,

The world's economy cripples into submission.

Loved ones stare at one another through stained windows

Growing tensions ripping families apart

Unemployment shadows blue skies in devilish hues

Depression suffocates the heartbroken; unconsciousness eternal.

Amid dwindling expectations, how does one find hope in the world?
What will it take to really live and love again?

For now, we can cling to possibility, a brighter world ahead;

Inflamed by internal hope and love cradled in one's heart

Enlightened by actions of integrity, faith and truth…

That will drive out the perverse darkness of this generation.

Descent - Tim Dibey

There are descent into the darkness
we search for a light.
The light, the light

Yearning for comfort in the air
pleasuring fortete
Fear is our only friend

We make our way deeper
till our rope is stretched taught
is this the end?

A hand a hand reaches mine
relief like a waterful
washes over me

I'm not alone
the cavern is filled with souls
lost broken tangled and exhausted
Led to hand to hand we form a chain
an unbreakable connection
Strength in numbers
Together we are the light
We are the hope
Together we will be ok

DESCENT

Jim Dukes

Through our descent into the darkness
We search for a light
THE light, ANY light.

Yearning for comfort in the air
Pleasantries fade
Fear is our only friend.

We make our way deeper
Til our rope is stretched taut
Is this the end?

A HAND! A hand reaches mind.
Relief like a waterfall
Washes over me.

I'm not alone.
The cavern is filled with souls
Hurt, broken, tangled and exhausted

Hand to Hand to Hand we form a chain
An unbreakable connection
Strength in numbers

Together, we are the light
We are the hope
Together we will be ok.

Crisis - Whats New   —Tim Dlog

Fuckn been there
A life of crisis and fear
Beatings abuse neglect

Death close calls - no answer
Fuck you death
Blasts, water, falls, crashes

Suicide failure - sobriety
Therapy helps talking writing feeling
New hope how long will it last

Stay home, Netflix, feed?
Is that really a crisis?
I'm alive, Fuckn been there

CRISIS – WHAT'S NEW?

Jim Dukes

Fuckn' been there
A life of crisis and fear
Beatings, abuse, neglect

Death. So many close calls – no answer
Fuck you death!
Explosions, drowning, falling, crashes

Suicide failure – Sobriety
Therapy helps. Talking, writing, feeling.
New hope. How long will it last?

Stay home, Netflix, food?
Is that really a crisis for me?
I'm alive, fuckn' been there.

Creativisty Dysmorphia - The Diary

I suck
The work I create is so flawed
Why do I try?

Why do you compliment me?
Can't yo see the lighting is off in the corner
Wy did i accept your money?

I cought the image
I felt the power of it
So what there are better photogs out there

I will remain obscure
Files on my computer never seen
I suck

CREATIVITY DYSMORPHIA

Jim Dukes

I suck
The work I create is so flawed
Why do I try?

Why do you compliment me?
Can't you see the light is off in the corner?
Why do I accept your money?

I caught the image
I felt the power of it
So what? There are better photographers out there.

I will remain obscure.
Files on my computer never seen.
I suck.

the Calling — Jin D10

- S200ft Away Salvation
- All this idle like gnawing my soul
- Playing movies of trauma death and fear

- My mind want shut it off
- It calls to me - my salvation
- The cold sudsy fried of years past

- Two isles of cold happies in the middle of nutrition
- I hear them my mind screams for release
- Happy bubbles of forget on my tongue

- So my past dreus me apart as I smile for you
- fourteen years sober want be ruined by
- S20g Away - salvation

THE CALLING

Jim Dukes

5,280 feet away - salvation.
All this idle time gnawing at my soul
Playing movies of trauma, death and fear.

My mind can't shut it off
It calls to me – my salvation
The cold, sudsy friends of years past.

Two isles of cold happiness in the middle of nutrition
I hear them. My mind screams for release.
Happy bubbles of forget on my tongue.

My past tears me apart as I smile for you
Fourteen years sober won't be ruined
5,280 feet away – salvation.

SEXUAL REPRESSION, BARRIER TO RACIAL EQUALITY

Jim Dukes

Ending racial inequality in America begins with brutal conversation. Sorry my black friends, white people are not emotionally equipped for this dialogue and subsequent problem solving.

Why?

A medium-sized group of sober white Americans cannot sit in a room and have an honest, open conversation about how good it feels to receive oral sex from their partner, or how she likes her hair pulled when he's behind her, or how he likes her to peg him occasionally, or that sometimes he can't get it up.

We repress those conversations about all the sexual things in life that make us feel great, because we feel shame, guilt and fear of judgment. It's inexcusable that our white culture has this disconnect regarding expressing sexual love, joy and ecstasy.

Thanks, organized religion!

My black friends, as you look to white people to help solve inequality, understand that, if we aren't comfortable speaking out loud about something pleasurable and universal, like how good an orgasm feels, how can we formulate the words to express why we feel afraid of some black people in a meeting, business or social setting or in our neighborhoods?

I think people want to talk, but revert to anger. This is an ineffective umbrella emotion under which people most times hide their real feelings.

Why?

Mostly, it's the lack of opportunity and experience in having honest conversations, even about the things that make us feel great.

White people, we need to mature as communicators, listen and talk without shame and help solve racial equality.

REAR VIEW

Lori Myers

Dangling, twisting, swaying
Chaotic motions mimic reality
Meaningful 3-D symbols
Joyous memories replaced.

Graduation tassel proudly displayed
My colors are better than yours
No honors, just made it out
So many years ago.

Glistening angel protects me
Guardian on the road
She knows my travels well
Always with me.

Rear view ornaments
Precious moments of life
Today hangs an N95
Joyous memories replaced.

TAYLOR MADE

Lori Myers

Taylor made everyone feel loved with his kind words, soft tone, and gentle spirit.

He so wanted to please others, but death left big holes in his heart. His music told his real story – pain and loss.

At 25, Taylor found his first true love. Grace filled much of the void. She was kindred, but wrestled the same demons.

It seemed he'd found that 'one' to pull him back from lonely, dark places.

Barely a year since they said, "I do." They found their rhyme – his music, her cats, their drugs. Heartache not comforted by words was eased by the numbing effects of Xanax.

Then came the paralyzing pandemic – fear, uncertainty, death. Pounded with constant reminders of a world out of control. No job, no help, little self-worth.

When he laid his head down that night was the dose to soothe or was it planned as the final escape? Damn it, we'll never know.

Worry replaced by mourning. Uncertainty replaced by finality. The sting is strong and anger deep as we struggle to understand WHY.

A mother shouldn't have to bury her 29-year-old son; a brother shouldn't say goodbye this soon, nor should a woman be a widow at thirty.

There's some comfort in knowing Taylor's battle is done. He left us many precious memories of his overflowing love for family.

His lyrics left us the roadmap of his heart.

RIP "Taylor Made" – you will "make it" as our angel in heaven!

UNPRECEDENTED

Lori Myers

Stay safe
Stay at home
Shelter in place

Hotspots, outbreaks
Jobs lost, food lines
Daily death toll

Birthdays without cakes
Births without celebration
Death without mourners

Contentment replaced with Chaos
Facts replaced with Fear
Journalism replaced with Opinionism

New norm, REALLY?

"WHY DON'T MY WAR STORIES COUNT?

Lori Myers

In middle school, I was looked down upon because my parents were factory workers. I couldn't afford to join ski club or summer at Wellesley Island.

Class shame.

In high school, I joined teenage motherhood - stereotyped as illiterate, poor, immoral. My doctor told me to have lots of babies so I could get more welfare.

Moral shame.

What could I amount to having come from working stock with a baby on my hip by 16? To overcome belittling characterizations meant to keep me 'in my place.' I worked hard at my career. Then I hit a wall because I lacked a college degree.

Intellectual shame.

My children's father was shot and killed by a New York State Trooper. This painful tragedy suggested abuse of power and questioned law enforcement's practice of 'shoot to kill'. The loss was exaggerated by social bashing following an article praising the officer's heroic efforts to stop a criminal.

Societal shame.

Now I'm expected to feel guilty about my skin color. My voice stifled because I don't fit the narrative of oppression. My color gave me a vail to hide behind, but it didn't afford me privilege. I didn't escape false perceptions or painful words that never considered my character or my heart. I am descendent of an indentured servant, sharecroppers, factory workers.

Race shame.

Struggle is struggle; pain is pain; loss is loss;
No matter the color of one's skin!

LOVE IS...

Lori Myers

... broad enough shoulders to carry the burden
   yet soft enough to cradle a loved one

... a touch that can soothe a frightened heart
... a smile that can warm the darkest places

... strong enough to protect and defend
   yet gentle enough to feel safe and secure in

... listening with genuine interest
... compassion with no bond to pride

... eyes that speak without using words
   yet unafraid to shed a tear when heart is touched

... a sense of humor that can bring a smile to anyone
... decisions and direction guided by integrity

... speaking with conviction and truth
   yet never missing an opportunity to say something kind

... freely given with no expectation or a return or personal gain
... the essence of humankind, need now more than ever!

THE CORONA COASTER

Amy Campbell Pratt

"Please keep your hands and feet inside the car at all times," calls the announcer as we settle in.

The danger and admission price is extremely high for this ride. Lost wages, lost careers, potential death.

Won't find this in the amusement parks. Disney's been closed for months, only the third time in its history.

Welcome to the Corona Coaster.

"RIDE AT YOUR OWN RISK!"

Wait! What!

"Hold on tight, here we go."

Clack, clack, clack up a massive mountain of dead bodies, past refrigerator trucks turned morgues, through the masked mob at Costco and failed leadership.

WHEEEEEEEE, careening at high speeds into grief so palpable we can taste it.

We feel the violent shifts of tectonic plates underneath the rickety tracks. At any moment, we could derail. We grip hard the lap bar with our gloved hands.

We don't have a choice. We are all on this ride together.

We hold on to the infinite possibility that with every bump, bruise and shake comes a shift, a new corner, a potential end.

It's the Corona Coaster. Wait! When can we get off?

Miles in with arms flung high, collectively we surrender to the ride, leaning into the curves as one screaming voice.

These ups and downs spreading panic through our minds without apology. Our bodies unhinged...

Us warriors of control lost this battle. And that's okay. Just lean in... Feel the fear. Feel the changes... release control. Enjoy the next ride!

COVID-19

Amy Campbell Pratt

New normal

Pivot

Covid-19

Buzzwords of the 21st century No end in sight

Invisible masks become visible straps around our ears No time for tears

Only fears remain.

Where do we go from here?

Get up and do it again

Again and again...

The axis of our existence Shifts

Into unimaginable rifts Of grief.

Hands clasped tightly together adorned in latex gloves

We push and we shove.

Leaders emerge in crowded streets

Chanting no justice, no peace...

Awaken us from our dream... rather a nightmare it seems

Humanity seeps into potholes underneath our feet

Towns, countries, parishes collectively weep...

This is our new normal, as we struggle to pivot, in the movement and era of Covid-19

521

PIVOT

Amy Campbell Pratt

Grasping for breath, no life remains.

Gone from our bodies the pain.
Carted off to refrigerated trucks,

keeping us plump 'Till boxes can be made

To take us to our final resting place.

Don't weep for us
Please
Pivot Instead

Change the course of history

We are a grief stricken lot.

There is no doubt.

Not a utopian spot to be found

In hallowed ground.

This once promise land of hope and prosperity
Is one government check away from bankruptcy.

Pivot

We must
Or go hungry

Trying for the American dream

This is our new normal, as we struggle to pivot, in the movement and
era of Covid-19

NEW NORMAL

Amy Campbell Pratt

Turn your can't into cans

Develop new plans in the midst of this earthquake...
A new normal exists in the quiet that persists...

No rushing to extra curricular activities

Cooking from home with groceries

Delivered right to your door.
For now... less is so much more

Sit with your family while you can
Hold each others' hands. Say grace, give thanks...

Renew your passions in jobless days and slow pace.

Remember with delight the dreams you once had ...the games you used
to play.

Step into the new normal, put down your beer

Self-medication only perpetuates your fear.

Lean into change.

Take this time to grow

Plant your garden reap what you sow.

Compassion is sure to emerge out of the chaos and hate

Breathe deeply while your lungs still allow
Let love envelop you and quiet the crowds;
Step boldly into the new normal as the superheroes we were created
to be.

Do Vote! Use YOUR voice.

Don't just follow mindlessly any orange clowns.

JUST BREATHE LOVE

Amy Campbell Pratt

Our world is in the middle of one huge panic attack, we can't catch our breath. Where fear reigns, love wanes.

The universe litters our paths with giant billboards - Covid-19, hate speech and Potus 45. Shallow breathe, our cause and effect.

Anger and hate constrict our ability to breathe, our ability to live in peace, our ability to love...

The cycle will continue until we create lasting change, lasting love, collectively breathing in the light so we can drown out darkness.

Breathe in for 4, out for 4.

Breathe in Love, Exhale Fear.

Breathe in Surrender, Exhale Control.

Love is Surrender, Fear is Control.

With each deep breath, we release love and light into the world; the more love and light, the less fear, anger and darkness.

The universe constantly reminds us to get back to basics.

Let us respond.

Let us love ourselves, so we can love each other.

Just breathe!

MUSIC COMING, VIRUS THING

Glenn Proctor

With warning, chaos came, swift with intensity, causing
Dire interruptions, world as one in deadly woe, without clarity
Hurt and fear spreading, black plastic filling without ceremony;
Humanity's thin ice exposed, yet home is safe, a walled sanctuary.
Still pain endures, slows rush and limits millions, weak and strong.
What is this, virus thing, unforgiving, biting colors without kisses?
Pushing grief behind glass or markers at six, creating rash theories
Curiosity circles without handshakes, trust or knowing all.

As hope potion, the popular slogan proclaims, "we're together" -
But without finding first the sick of our least in dismissed places;
Usual bigs swallow big dollars; little fish drown in economic abyss;
So embellish not the word fair, saying equal is equal, this time or ever;
Reality's an unforgiving binged show of survival, anxiety and doubt.
Yet, hope for good endings abound with masked givers and doers;
Their Serenity Prayers flowing in 12-hour shifts and food banks.
Without rest, with tears, they alone comfort when sick eyes close.

One day something will happen, but what is this thing called normal?
A different society perhaps born, smacking some, pleasing others;
Grief and uncertainty will live; yet ideas bloom like morning glories;
Change will find us, new tunes playing without distance or shelter.

REALITY LOST

Glenn Proctor

Forgive me if I don't comprehend all folks in these days
Passing the unmasked, others with noses and mouths hidden
Standing apart, curious for reality or none. The farce lives,
Killing them, not us, close and mysterious, yet of no concern;
Just find our busy familiar, burning restless days and nights
Seeking quick return to primary drugs - work, money and play.

Some speak empathy, but humanity's decency bucket leaks
Caution words careen off closed buildings seeking outside air,
Bits of leadership blow away unheard, safety remains chaotic;
With some believing, others uncertain, still others unfazed.
As much as hope folks whisper prayers and speak aloud;
Truth is individual, each fish swimming in different water.

Why do our tears not fill oceans, our grief unanimous?
Seems soft screaming never spreads between our two oceans
Apathy flying like shooting stars, scorching truth and equality;
Between gratitude, grief and return, we all wait for the unknown.
The listening go one way, the unhearing seek another truth
Amid crisis, we stand divided. Together is just hope, a bad dream still.

WHO'S ENTITLED TO PRIVILEGE?

Glenn Proctor

Never felt entitled, being better, above others, or best;
Privilege, word never spoken or thought, even in certain years
When subtle respect and fleeting titles flourished as reality;
When scrappin' and scrapin' lingered, hiding in my shadows.

Never had polished spoons, *right* history or birth name; yet
Revenge scripted is damn cool; hopin' and hustlin' in plain sight.
Should I be sometimes ass like others, the risky unmasked?
No, not wanting to catch death drops flying in uncertain winds.

Privileged thinking never came, yet you shower it like summer rain
Believing *something* allows you to shun listening, proclaim normal
To finding your daily must haves; poking rule and consequence.
Let bodies stack. Is humanity's finish line closer than imagined?

Do all wish to gather again like ants; seeking rush from shelter time?
Bits of patience ensue, others claw out; doors swing open to swarms;
Let's get back to the grind. Distance and health warnings ignored.
Beware of what? Protestors with guns boost privilege called *rights*.
Yet, life is not yours or mine alone; the mask you wear may save us both.
Not expecting us *together as friends;* just wanting to reach tomorrow.

SEE

Glenn Proctor

Don't like what I see in bathroom mirror with water drops

Adrift eyes, itchy gray beard mashed, days abandoned;

Mouth night sour, needing water, seeking to produce

Morning positives before profanity, grief and news

Dribbling negatives. Short silence attempts gratitude;

Yet inside sounds, unheard and frightening, scream;

Muted words sprint the hills up from my throat.

Time is passing, quickly like dirt shoveled on graves

During thunder, when virus kills bodies strong and

Weak. Tongues silent as disrupters rage with guns;

Proclamations push healing, coming in another morning.

Why did I not achieve more? Why am I afraid now?

Second-guessing the rare life, pride and connections;

Enough was better than good for decades of decisions,

Notoriety, chances, charm, without big fame, big riches.

Homeless coins not needed on rainbow morning, yet age

Flows steady, each year pushing against hopes of

One more game, wearing blues upright, bounding stairs for sex;

Sitting left seat high over autumn patches of closed farms.

Truth is, shiny mirrors sing no hallelujahs, or comfort;

Uncertainty smashes worn traditions with anxious glee.

At times, I hate you, mirror. Silence, truth; pure and absolute;

'Though when I wake, I'll look away as you clean your soul.

Billions of humans sat on life's normal wall

Now millions of humans are fighting sick call

Masked workers, responders, both women and men

Need help putting economy and sanity back together again.

Thanks and apologies to Humpty Dumpty and James William Elliott, 1870

GOOD DAYS AHEAD

Glenn Proctor

The last poem of this series must not be so dire,
Together we're world caught in condition of mire.
We're coming back stronger when timing is right;
Grit, grace, patience and work will lessen this plight.

Ahead days will be different, our normal brand new;
Virus, vision and vaccine are changers; we must change too.
Be groups of saviors, helping nurses who toil before sun
They grieve and work steady, long days yet not done.

At this time of hurt and renewal; uncertainty so real;
Need connection and chatter, make known how we feel.
Be anxious, yet hopeful; busy with trust and belief
In life's scheme of history and years, this situation is brief.
View the world in its beauty; new or old music is sound.
Today is a blessing, head up with feet on solid ground.
Think positive thoughts; end worries of normal and gloom.
Children still laugh and play; red and white roses still bloom.

LONGING & REGRET

Kimberly Shelton

A phone call, received from someone who cares. A visit, from anyone will do. Meaningful conversation, a kiss on the cheek, the touch of a hand, a hug. So are the gifts most longed for by the dying.

Time: the most precious of all commodities when in your final days. It was the only request he had of me and I did not deliver. Why? Because it was the one thing I didn't have to give. I was too busy with the minutiae of the mundane. Inundated with the all-encompassing, onerous, insignificant-but-necessary responsibilities of my life, dictated to me by the harsh taskmaster of my "to-do" list.

"Please, when you get a chance, could you give me a call?" he implored in his voicemail. And at the time, I had no way of knowing those would be his final words to me, the last time I would ever hear his voice. And now, I am reeling with the repercussions of my inaction.

Regret... such a punishing pill to swallow, or rather should I say, choke on. Why didn't I... call him more often, spend quality time with him, show him how much his friendship meant to me?

And now, I am asking myself... "what could you have done differently had you known he would be dead in a month," that you would never see or hear from him again? And what I wouldn't give to gaze into his eyes once more, to see his sweet smile, to feel the touch of his hand in mine, to hear his voice, to tell him how much he meant to me, how much I cared, to say goodbye.

But, *I DIDN'T. HAVE. TIME.* So the opportunity to do so vanished; was stolen from me by the invisible Covid-19. And now, I am left lamenting his death with the weight of the undone on my conscience.

Time... given to everyone, but promised to no one. What do you need to say or do NOW?

MEANING

Kimberly Shelton

During the quarantine, I decided to take a time out; a purposeful withdrawal from life as I knew it. When the frenetic activity abruptly ended, I began paying attention to the everyday. And in so doing, became aware of a plethora of things that prior to I had barely noticed.

The English proverb, "the best things in life are free" began to take on true meaning for me. Before, the things I was oblivious to or found insignificant, were suddenly deemed to be of the most utmost importance.

I discovered they created within me a profound sense of pleasure that had previously been unbeknownst to me. I began to feel peaceful. And, as I embraced contentment, I realized I had found meaning in the heretofore meaningless, joy in the ordinary, significance in simplicity. It amazed me that I hadn't been attentive to these treasures before and now they were priceless to me.

Inundated with the trivial, I never took the time to discover the delightful. It took a pandemic to reveal to me what is truly invaluable in life.

I am exceedingly grateful for the gift of awareness I've received. And, the best part?

The things that bring me the most joy truly **are** free. And now I know this experientially.

LIFE

Kimberly Shelton

Life… so precious, yet so fragile. Could be ripped away at any moment for any reason. Expected, as in the case of a long-term illness or unexpected, as in the case of an accident or pandemic.

When will my expiration date be? The instant I cease to exist. The moment I melt into the nothingness from whence I came. Back to the ether, my essence no more.

When I contemplate my own death, it arouses within me feelings of fear, anxiety, panic. Have I done everything I wanted/needed to do? I have not. And, I am struck with the realization that I need to get my shit together, **PRONTO!**

That should my expiration date be tomorrow, I will have left behind a whole host of things that have not been taken care of. Loose ends, still dangling, leaving a mess for others to clean up behind me.

My affairs are not in order. No plan in place for my wishes. No one appointed to carry them out. Should they have instructions? They don't.

But truly, the contemplation of my demise begs the bigger questions:

What legacy do I want to leave? Will I feel as though I have accomplished everything I set out to do? And, if so, exactly what is it that I've set out to do? Anything? What's on my bucket list or do I even have one? What are my dreams and goals?

What would make me happy? Do I want to have peace and joy in my life and if so, how will I accomplish that? What is my purpose? Why am I here? What do I have to contribute, to give? What do I want to leave behind, if anything?

How will I measure whether or not my life has been a success? Have I filled it with the meaningful and if so, what does that look like?

What brings me joy? What's going to matter in the end?

F.E.A.R.

Kimberly Shelton

I remember how I felt as I watched the World Trade Center Towers imploding, creating within me a sense of helplessness; an inability to protect myself against the unknown. The unseen enemy was potentially lurking around any and every corner, poised to strike at any moment of its choosing, unsuspected and imperceptible to me.

As a result, my feelings of vulnerability heightened to a degree I had never experienced. I suddenly realized there was **NO** safe place to go, that I could be targeted at any moment or at any place on the planet.

Fear welled up inside, gripping me with its vice-like tentacles of terror, threatening to ambush me with the inconceivable, the unthinkable.

Enveloped with panic, I was petrified, unable to feel safe anywhere, not unlike the feelings I have now about the pandemic. If I am exposed to the virus, there's a real possibility of my demise.

Will I become a victim of the invisible that could take my life at any time?

Fear, in society's terms, stands for **False Evidence Appearing Real**. For me, it stands for **Ferociously Ensnaring** my **Ability** to **Reason**.

With that realization, I created this motto: *LIVE WHILE YOU'RE STILL ALIVE!*

SAVOR EVERY SECOND OF LIFE while you can still walk, talk, breathe and have your five senses. While you can savor the scrumptiousness of a sundae, be mesmerized by a magnificent full moon, revel in rays of sunshine warming your body, melt into the embrace of your lover, whisper the sweet nothings someone special longs to hear, take comfort in your cat's contented purr, experience the exuberance of your dog's wagging tail each time you enter the room, feel the fresh fallen rain on your face, hear the symphony of owls hooting in the night or marvel at a majestic waterfall.

Whatever brings you joy, do it. Act now before you're out of time and the opportunity passes you by.

DO what needs to be done! **SAY** what needs to be said! **LISTEN** to what you need to hear! **SEE** what you need and want to see. **BECOME** who you were meant to be. **MITIGATE** the meaningless. **INTENSIFY** the important. **DO IT NOW!**

LUXURIOUS LOVE

Kimberly Shelton

When the coronavirus first hit, I freaked out. Never having given things like germs and viruses a second thought, I now found myself frantically Cloroxing every doorknob, "every everything" in my house and car.

Also, taking my temperature several times a day to see if it had spiked became my new norm.

After panicking for a week or so, I realized I could no longer live with the constant and inescapable fear of the unknown… the unseen virus. The "what if's" were too much to bear and were beginning to take a toll.

The uncertainty, the not knowing, was getting the best of me. I knew this was not sustainable. Every day was a battle within my mind… I thought of nothing else.

Then, one morning I awoke to the coos of a mourning dove ushering in a new day. The feeling I received from this simple, yet soothing sound, was incredibly comforting to my soul.

As I lay in bed and thoughts of fear began bubbling up again, I decided to focus on the peace the dove had given me. It occurred to me that I could *choose* to think thoughts of love rather than thoughts of fear.

As I diverted my attention back to the dove's song, I began to contemplate all the things in my life that elicit feelings of being loved instead of feelings of being afraid. My decision was to focus on everything that gives me comfort, peace, tranquility and bliss.

The result: I am learning to pause, to sit in the moment, to allow myself to feel and experience bliss, to not rush with hurried abandon to the next task.

Now, I stop, recognizing the moment for the gift that it is, permitting myself to revel in the luxuriousness of love.

WHAT HAVE WE LOST?

Trish Stukbauer

The online tickers count what we have lost in morbid, flashing lights.

More than 280,000 and counting irreplaceable lives.

More than 20.5 million U.S. jobs lost in April alone.

More than 43 percent of small businesses believe they have less than 6 months until a permanent shutdown is unavoidable.

More than families who might take years to recover from the strain.

More than small businesses built by years of sacrifice that might never crawl out from under crushing economic blows.

Even more than individual lives.

We've lost time. We've lost the priceless opportunity to simply be together.

To throw a hat in the air at graduation amid the roaring cheers of classmates.

To playfully jostle to catch a bouquet as friends dash away with *Just Married* hastily scrawled across their rear window.

To laugh as children chase each other around a backyard birthday party.

To sing until we're hoarse as our favorite band explodes onto the stage.

To share a beverage with friends at a neighborhood cookout.

The chance for women and children at risk to seek a safe harbor away from home.

And those even more irreplaceable moments.

Hours spent lost in stories told by aging relatives in nursing homes.

Those final heart-wrenching minutes at the side of a loved one's hospital bed.

Hearing the first cries of a newborn grandchild.

Sharing coffee and conversation with a friend we didn't realize would be taken too soon.

That's what we've truly lost – and, what, we must now ask ourselves, has won?

COMING TOGETHER AGAIN?

Trish Stukbauer

Trails of smoke and spires of flame blazed across our TV screens on that fateful day.

Out of wreckage and thousands of broken lives, piece by piece, the world came together.

United by an unthinkable act that sparked worldwide fear.

Seeing not color, nor creed, nor gender, nor conviction; just humanity.

Coming together to combat evil on all fronts.

Gone all too soon.

Compassion faded.

Divisions returned with a vengeance.

Back to the real world.

That grew increasingly, violently divided.

Until...

An unthinking virus that sparked worldwide fear

Came not with smoke and flame.

But with the stealth of quiet breaths.

Made the world come together to care for the most vulnerable.

Emerging from the wreckage of thousands of broken lives.

Seeing not color, nor creed, nor gender, nor conviction; just humanity.

This time, will we learn?

Or will the divisions return?

WHAT HAVE WE GAINED?

Trish Stukbauer

When the world stopped turning for endless days and sleepless nights, we lost more than we imagined possible.

But, what did we gain?

Appreciation

For the knowledge that we are all connected.

For unsung heroes whose seemingly mundane toil was proven truly essential.

For perspective on who and what was not.

For family members who, even when near, were still too distant.

For friends whose laughter kept us sane.

For stolen conversations with strangers in places where we normally never would have paused.

For technology that facilitates human connection.

For the moments, large and small, that will be cherished when we can experience them again.

For handshakes and hugs.

For giving a fist bump to a stranger without flinching.

For the ability to work using both brawn and brains.

For freedoms taken all too easily.

For those who bravely stood, and those who fearlessly fought.

How long will all of it linger, once life inevitably goes on?

Contextomy!

Trish Stukbauer

is...

Too many truths in too few characters...

Hypocrisy exposed.

Lies rampant.

Paranoia pervasive.

Hatred misplaced.

Fears unfounded.

Panic widespread.

Needs unmet.

Lives shattered.

Faith questioned.

Mettle tested.

Strength revealed.

Character affirmed.

Prayers answered.

God omnipresent.

Did the world notice?

Or merely absorb the sound bite?

CAN LOVE CHANGE OUR WORLD?

Trish Stukbauer

"Man must evolve for all human conflict a method which rejects revenge, aggression and retaliation. The foundation of such a method is love."

- Martin Luther King, Jr.

All we need is love.

Love conquers all.

In songs, stories, poems and platitudes,

Love always triumphs.

Why not in our too real world?

In war-ravaged villages painted in stark shades of grey and red?

In an orphan's outstretched skeletal hands?

In bloodshot eyes of a child-woman battered by life and men?

In the streets of Seattle, torn apart by hatred and fear?

It's there.

Beyond the shrill voices.

In the eyes of a Marine lifting a child above the rubble.

On the shoulders of aid workers carrying food.

In the words of a social worker taking time to pray with a shattered victim.

In the subdued conversation of friends seeking to understand a fractured city.

Love is already changing our world.

We are just too focused on hatred to recognize it.

DREAMING IN COLOR

Andrea Towner

I have a dream…

A colorful dream with friends of all races, ethnicities and nationalities

A dream where we only see each other's humanity,

Appreciating our rich tapestry of skin tones, experiences and cultures;

Woven together tightly so we won't tear;

Bound with compassion, empathy, understanding…

Interwoven with warps completely covered with weft,

Individually fragile, but strong and balanced together.

Perhaps still, there will be fraying at the edges

Yet, with only a few loose threads on the periphery.

I don't believe this magic carpet is a myth,

I believe we are looming on the precipice of flight.

God doesn't play favorites and we're created in His image

And His image stretches imagination, His visage varied.

Loop your arms together, hold hands, share the smiles

We don't have to speak the same language to say volumes.

COLOR BLIND? NO, JUST TEMPORARY BLINDNESS

Andrea Towner

When my brother and I were small, our parents took us to see Santa at a Connecticut mall. We saw the jolly fellow and got in a long winding line where St. Nick was out of view.

By the time we got to the front of the line, Santa had changed shifts. Mom and Dad later told us they wondered if we would ask why Santa was now a black man – when clearly he was white when we first saw him.

We didn't say a word.

As a teen, we moved to Hilton Head, SC and I immediately became aware of the socioeconomic divide between the black kids who lived just off the island, riding buses to the public high school, and the wealthy white kids who drove Mercedes and BMWs to school. I didn't like what I saw and didn't feel like I fit in.

After moving to North Carolina as an adult, our first friends were a black family. We took pride in our son's best friends in elementary school being African-American, Asian American and Indian American. I thought we lived in a wonderful melting pot of equality.

It wasn't until the riots in Charlotte and around the country in 2016 that my eyes were truly opened to the inequality that still existed.

The blinders are off. I'm still seeing red (lines) four years later, making me feel an intense determination to see permanent change.

I will no longer remain silent or in the dark.

A PANDEMIC POEM

Andrea Towner

Although the view from my window is beautiful
My welcome mat has been withdrawn
Paper products are hard to procure
It's hugs I miss the most.

Smiles can't be seen behind the masks
Yet online conversations bridge the divide,
With back of hair and waist down ignored.
Can we truly all connect in the cloud?
It's ethereal and yet, substantial still.

Sitting still while Zooming from here to there
Every effort spent being present in the moment
Gratitude life's focal point; recognizing that good health,
Sunshine, spring flowers, high speed internet are daily gifts.

Call it staycation, nowhere to go, all day to get there
What day is it? What time is now? How long will this last?
Opportunity extends its open arms to us today
Listen and see, a prayer and encouragement for all.

IS IT TIME TO CHECK UNDER THE HOOD?

Diane Weekley

Seven weeks into the Pandemic, like a 1957 Chevrolet Bel Air convertible, some days I feel like I am cruising, other days I need my spark plugs replaced and a new distributor cap.

As I lay in the dawning between sleep and consciousness, a voice asked, "Is it time to check under the hood?"

In this era of COVID19, Newscasts and Updates create terrifying scenarios of sickness and fear with hope dangled in the form of a vaccine.

The Left and Right vie for credibility and political worldview prominence. To my husband checking under the hood means listening to the forecast, checking the metaphorical and meteorological weather, and confirming supply chains for meat and essential supplies. To other family members it means worst-case scenario prepping, six months of food, water, fuel and ammunition, and the imminent establishment of the Police State.

To me, it means maintaining a pulse on symptoms of disease and well–being. It means tuning in to the hearts and minds of those I care for: family, friends, colleagues and clients. It means doing my best to remain hopeful amidst ambiguity.

Battle weary, I maintain a healthy skepticism, and walk the tightrope between vaccine as "The Remedy" and the assertion everyone should buy an assault weapon.

If Ray Bradbury were writing today, what would he say about it? Fahrenheit 451 2020 where are you?

When you check under your hood, what do you find?

Will you allow it, accept it, affirm it with affection or decline to dance in the moment?

The choice is yours.

SPRING GREENEST GREEN

Diane Weekley

Spring greenest grass into Life!
Ignore desolation, repel inner strife.
Skies bluer than robin's egg hold heaven's arch,
And ceilingless dreams continue to march
Forth without hesitation.

Peek through the mists and sniff cold hard Truth.
Courage unheeded pollutes good Vermouth.
Ol' Dullahan rides seeking victims to bludgeon,
Uncertainty throws faith deep into dungeons
Unlocked, gates dangle wide open.

Leap greenest grass into Life!
Convert sequestration, enact as midwife.
Curiosity heals, transforms mournful days,
Suspend disbelief, escape epoch's malaise.
Love, pray, eat...Blaze.

JUST A BUNNY

Diane Weekley

Small daily rituals embed good habits. Coffee scents foster peace like a thurible that venerates an Alter. Not today. I sit in Papa Jack's old rocker in overwhelm. So much to do; yet here I sit.

High expectations, energy alarmingly flat.

"Be the rocker. Create a movement. Share your wisdom. Push it out!"

A load of Crap. What is my Word for Today? Breathe. Quiet the mind. I wait. Nothing. Get up and move. The trash needs dumping. It stinks.

It lay still as if sleeping, tiny left leg outstretched, paws curled inward, teeny ears flat against its crown, breathless on concrete. What creature is this? Breath escapes in a sigh.

A baby bunny. Just a bunny.

Bunnies abound this time of year. They hop and bop all over, munching on grass, fearlessly bounding from interest to interest. Curious, I scrutinize the white underbelly hair that thinly follows the curve of the tiny tummy. Still, like a soft stuffed animal turned to stone.

The white trash bag beckons as it leans against the red recycling bin. "Scoop it into the trash, it's just a bunny."

Expedience pooh-poohs reverence; arrogance throws life in the waste bin.

I scan the yard for a suitable resting place. A nearby shovel floats into my grasp. I dig in a haze of emotion. Gently cradled in a soft earthen tomb, I sprinkle dirt onto its belly. Tamped down, earth in place, I topple-test the River Red Concrete Edger that will mark its grave.

The unobserved grief of thousands compressed into eight disruptive weeks erupts in uncontrollable salty sobs.

There is no escaping grief, no magic pill to "make it all better." Grief knows no timetable, has no shelf life and comes without warning. Still, we must persevere and with compassion, bury our bunnies.

CURBSIDE PICKUP

Diane Weekley

Fifteen steps to work in my "fixer-up" means 50 projects vie for attention every morning. I hope I am up for the challenge.

"Need materials? Call ahead or order online." Starting small, I order light bulbs, Edison bulbs and potting soil.

First stop. Home Depot. It's the first time at The Home Depot since the stay-in-place order limited travel except for essential items. The parking lot, full of vehicles, shouts business as usual. Yellow daisies, pink petunias and blue hydrangeas splash color along the Garden Center fence. People load products into trucks. Blue-gloved hands pushing carts grab my attention. Half masks seclude smiles. Eyes that once welcomed strangers look away.

A first-time makeshift stanchion of yellow rope and two-by-four wooden posts weave a u-shaped lane to massive gliding doors. I ride around the lot and call as instructed, "Here for Curbside Pickup. Weekley."

I call, I ride. I wait. I park. I call a friend. Where is the pickup lane? I look for phantom sales associates. "Should I call again?" I park and put on a surgical mask. Grumbling, I bristle, "I'll get it myself."

In dim light, standing six-feet apart, shoppers form a 20-foot line to cashier stations adorned with plastic Sneeze Guards. A cart parked next to Customer Service offers an untidy array of gloves, a spray bottle and wipes.

I call to a woman in an orange apron. "What did you buy," she asks, frowning through her mask. "Your name," she calls, walking away.

What did I purchase here? "Uh, Edison bulbs, light bulbs. Weekley. Diane." "Is Weekley in the queue?" she calls, walking toward a locker.

I wonder if they got the order. Crud, I ordered potting soil too. Or, was that here or Walmart? Should I say something. My irritation rises. Customer service is terrible. I work to self-regulate.

"Damn virus," I mutter. Irritation turns to spontaneous sadness. Gloom permeates my space. With purchase in hand, I flee to the car. It's too late for another curbside pickup. I surrender.

Later, I pause to write a gratitude list. Stop the Insanity! Imagine the 'fixer-upper' as Old Tuscan Farmhouse in disguise. That I can live with… That I can love…Goodbye projects! Attitude adjustment complete.

LOVE'S TAR-FILLED PROMISE

Diane Weekley

Dark tar-filled Love wells up, clogs the throat

Emotions jammed together, damned together

This Promise built in desperation, certainty of exhortation,

    Secreted within the invincibility of youth.

This Promise

    To break the chains,

        Love forever,

            Never leave or forsake,

                Be savior to self and sons.

This promise made with true intent, true love, true desire, true heart,

    True heart, true blasphemy.

Every known thing, not true.

This Promise portending Utopian perfection, now brittle and bare

Made in recovery, ever hopeful, transformed to tears, salty, briny, bottomless.

Love exhausts me, lies brutally beaten, traumas compartmentalized, once

    Neatly boxed, labeled and stacked. Packaged in black and white.

Brimming, bursting with feed for the wolf.

Self-compassion, little willingness to forgive,

How will we ever reach across the divide?

ORIGINAL QUOTES, MADE TO LAST...

"Control your breath, incessantly focus on gratitude, experience moments of peace."

- Andrea Towner

"Optimism runs like a spring thaw, quenching summer's parch."

- Doreen Day

"Be courageous. Crack imagination's golden egg. Tell your raw truth. Write."

- Diane Weekley

"What you value comes to you. What you don't, you lose."

- Jeffrey Bryant

"Intentionally wander to evoke your essence."

- Lori Myers

"Want to make a real difference? Pray, love and then stand up."

- Trish Stukbauer

"Become a warrior within to outrun fear. If not, fear is your conqueror."

- Glenn Proctor

"Your journey is a carefully conducted orchestra, there is nothing *RANDOM* about it."

- Amy Campbell Pratt

"Persistence will get you far, faith will take you the rest of the way."

- Carla A. Carlisle

"Everything that happens is orchestrated by the Universe for your highest good."

- Kimberly Shelton

"Strive to be a light that brings darkness trembling to its knees."

- Sara Dir

"Don't sit there contemplating the lint in your navel. Live with purpose."

- Jim Dukes

"I'm alive, so I might as well keep trying."

- Lizz Baxter

Can we cling to hope amid crisis?

Can we recover from a pandemic, economic upheaval and racial unrest?

Can we one day become the nation we were meant to be, where equality, truth and empathy rise above color, money and power?

We must.

We're uncertain when you are reading this book - in late 2020 or months and years beyond. Thank you for reading.

This book is our truthful reminder of a two-month period in 2020 when our communities, our states, America and the world were in the midst of a triple crisis – a growing pandemic, surging economic loss and racial unrest.

The goal was to share experiences and perspective while sowing truth, transparency and words of hope. Some pieces are raw and emotional, depicting the writer's mood or specific circumstance during this period.

We hope life, especially in America, has changed for the better since May and June 2020 when most of these short stories, opinions and poems were written.

If not, we urge each of you to keep learning, keep listening, keep striving to make our country a healthy, equitable and economically rewarding place for all citizens. We must.

Another nod to WRITING BOOTCAMP Charlotte members who challenged themselves to participate in this project: Lizz Baxter, Jeffrey Bryant, Carla A. Carlisle, Doreen Day, Sara Dir, Jim Dukes, Lori Myers, Amy Campbell Pratt, Kimberly Shelton, Trish Stukbauer, Andrea Towner and Diane Weekley.

Thank you.

Glenn Proctor

Notes

Notes

CPSIA information can be obtained
at www.ICGtesting.com
Printed in the USA
LVHW111133251120
672638LV00006B/621